# Discovering SuperCroc

# Discovering
# SuperCroc

By Pamela Rushby

NATIONAL GEOGRAPHIC

WASHINGTON, D.C.

Founded in 1888, the National Geographic Society is one of the largest nonprofit scientific and educational organizations in the world. It reaches more than 285 million people worldwide each month through its official journal, NATIONAL GEOGRAPHIC, and its four other magazines; the National Geographic Channel; television documentaries; radio programs; films; books; videos and DVDs; maps; and interactive media. National Geographic has funded more than 8,000 scientific research projects and supports an education program combating geographic illiteracy.

For more information, please call
1-800-NGS-LINE (647-5463) or write to the following address:

National Geographic Society
1145 17th Street N.W.
Washington, D.C. 20036-4688
U.S.A.

Visit us online at www.nationalgeographic.com/books

For information about special discounts for bulk purchases, please contact
National Geographic Books Special Sales at ngspecsales@ngs.org

For rights or permissions inquiries, please contact National Geographic
Books Subisidiary Rights: ngbookrights@ngs.org

Copyright © 2007 National Geographic Society

Text revised from *SuperCroc* in the National Geographic Windows on Literacy program from National Geographic School Publishing, © 2004 National Geographic Society

All rights reserved. Reproduction of the whole or any part of the contents without written permission from the publisher is prohibited.

Published by National Geographic Society. Washington, D.C. 20036

Design by Project Design Company
Photo Editor: Annette Kiesow
Project Editor: Anita Schwartz

Printed in the United States

**Library of Congress Cataloging-in-Publication Data**

Rushby, Pamela.
  Discovering SuperCroc / by Pamela Rushby.
      p. cm. -- (National Geographic science chapters)
  ISBN 978-1-4263-0186-5 (library)
1. Crocodiles, Fossil. 2. Dinosaurs. I. Title.
QE862.C8R87 2007
567.9'8--dc22

2007007906

**Photo Credits**
Front Cover: © Raul Martin; Spine, Endsheet: © Theo Allofs/zefa/CORBIS; 2-3: © Joshua Ets-Hokin/CORBIS; 6: © Will Burgess/Reuters/CORBIS; 7, 26-27 (bottom): © National Geographic Image Collection; 8-9 © Don Foley; 10: © Michael Rothman; 12: © Michael S. Lewis/CORBIS; 12 (inset), 13: © Luke Jurevicius; 14, 17, 23: © Courtesy of Project Exploration; 15, 16, 19, 22, 24, 25, 33: © C. Mike Hettwer courtesy of Project Exploration; 20: © Paul Sereno and Carol Abraczinskas courtesy of Project Exploration; 26 (top): © Bill Bachman Photography; 26 (middle): © Oxford Scientific/Jupiter Images; 28: © Ralph A. Clevenger/CORBIS; 30-31: © Ray Carson/UF News Bureau; 32, 35: © Rick Bowmer/Associated Press; 34: © David Gray/Reuters/CORBIS.

Endsheets: Too close to a crocodile!

# Contents

A young boy rests on a model of SuperCroc on display at the Australian Museum.

# What Is a Croc?

Crocodiles are large reptiles that live in warm, wet, swampy places. With their powerful tails and armorlike skin, they move fast both on land and in water. Their hearts and lungs let them stay underwater for more than an hour if they must.

The Nile crocodile lives along the Nile River and other watery habitats in Africa.

Crocodiles are carnivores. This means they eat meat. Crocodiles are known for their sneak attacks. They hide, then catch animals that pass nearby with their huge jaws. You wouldn't want to get too close to a crocodile!

Today, the biggest crocodiles grow to about 20 feet (6 meters) long. However, 110 million years ago, much larger crocodiles lived.

This ancient croc with its massive tail was one of the largest and most powerful crocs to ever roam the Earth.

*Sarcosuchus* drags a Hadrosaur under the water much like a present day crocodile drowns its prey.

# Chapter 1

# SuperCroc

The first scientists who found bones of this giant animal named it *Sarcosuchus imperator*, meaning "flesh crocodile emperor." But that name is a mouthful, so scientists also call this ancient croc SuperCroc. This amazing creature lived when dinosaurs roamed the Earth, millions of years ago.

SuperCroc was two times the size of the largest crocs today. Scientists think it was 40 feet (12 meters) long—about as long as a school bus. It may have weighed as much as 20,000 pounds (9,000 kilograms)!

**Sahara Desert**

**Africa**

Sand dunes cover much of the Sahara, the largest desert in the world.

SuperCroc lived in northern Africa. It lived in an area that is now part of the Sahara, a very large desert. Like all deserts, the Sahara is a very dry and sandy place. But a croc needs water to live. How could one live in the desert?

Over 100 million years ago, the Sahara was an area of lakes, rivers, and forested plains.

The Sahara looked very different 110 million years ago. In fact, it was not a desert at all. It was more like the Everglades in Florida. There were rivers, lakes, plants, and trees. Many different animals, including dinosaurs, lived there.

Paul Sereno carefully digs out fossil material buried in the rocky desert.

# Chapter 2

# Finding SuperCroc

In 1993, Paul Sereno, a scientist from the University of Chicago, began a series of expeditions to the Sahara. He traveled with other scientists in search of dinosaur fossils. Fossils are the hardened remains of living things that died millions of years ago. These scientists, called paleontologists, hoped to find fossils that would help them learn about the past.

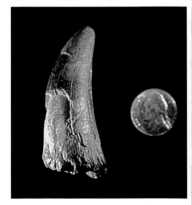

**A fossilized SuperCroc tooth is shown next to a nickel for size comparison.**

Sereno's team digs out the skulls of two giant crocs they uncovered in the sandstone.

It is not easy to work in the desert. Temperatures can hit 125°F (52°C) and there are sandstorms. Travel is difficult and jeeps and trucks often get stuck in the sand. In spite of this, the scientists were successful. On the 1997 expedition, Sereno and his team collected tons of dinosaur fossils. They also found the giant skull of an adult crocodile-like animal.

The fossil jaws of a giant croc lie in the sands of a desert region in Niger, a country in northwestern Africa.

Sereno believed that there were even more fossils to uncover at different sites in the desert. So, he planned a return trip for the fall of 2000 to continue his search. This time, he brought along five Land Rovers and enough supplies to stay for four months. Sereno and his team began to dig at the same place where the croc skull had been found three years before.

Right away, the team found something they knew was not a dinosaur. They found a very large jawbone. Its shape was very different from dinosaur fossils they had found before. This fossil was the jaw of SuperCroc.

The scientists could not believe what they had found. The jaw was longer than most people on the team. Paul Sereno said it was "about the biggest I've ever seen." He knew that he and his team had made a very important discovery.

Paul Sereno carefully brushes sand from the fossil of a giant croc.

The giant croc's head was separated from its neck. As the team continued to dig, they found more of SuperCroc's bones. They now had about half of the bones, but some were still missing. Sereno and his team did not know what a whole SuperCroc looked like. How could they find out?

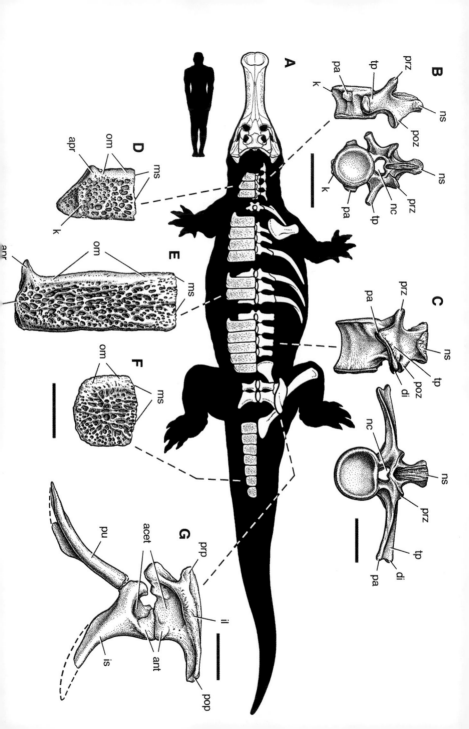

# Chapter 3

# SuperCroc Math

Paul Sereno knew a lot about dinosaurs. He knew the bones he had found were like dinosaur bones. But he knew they were also like crocodile bones. Sereno decided to ask someone who knew about crocodiles for help. He called a crocodile expert named Brady Barr. Together they studied all of the bones. They could tell from the bones' shapes that this animal was like a crocodile—a very large crocodile!

◄ This illustration by Paul Sereno shows the SuperCroc bones that he and his team found. It also shows how a modern-day adult human (upper left) compares in size with the giant croc.

The scientists wanted to know what SuperCroc looked like when it was alive. They wanted to know how big it was. To figure out the size of SuperCroc's body, they needed more information. They decided to compare SuperCroc's bones with the bones of crocodiles that live today. Then they used math to figure out how large SuperCroc was.

Known as the "Gator Doc," field specialist Brady Barr studies crocodiles and alligators.

These are the fossil remains of SuperCroc's teeth.

Sereno and Barr measured the length of the giant skull that the team found. Then they measured the length of skulls of crocodiles that live today. They used these two measurements to estimate, or make a best guess, about how big SuperCroc might have been.

**Paul Sereno and Brady Barr compare the skull of today's crocodile with SuperCroc's jawbones.**

The giant skull was 6 feet (2 meters) long. That was more than two times the size of the modern crocodile skull. Sereno and Barr measured the length and size of all of the bones they found. They used this information to make an even better estimate of SuperCroc's size. They thought that SuperCroc must have been more than two times as long as today's crocodiles, about 40 feet (12 meters) long!

The next step was to figure out how much SuperCroc weighed. So, Paul Sereno and Brady Barr found information about how much today's crocodiles weigh. Then they used math to estimate how much SuperCroc probably weighed. They estimated that SuperCroc weighed about nine tons. That's about 18,000 pounds (8,100 kilograms)!

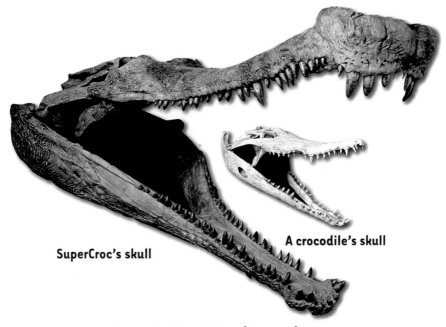

**A crocodile's skull**

**SuperCroc's skull**

SuperCroc's skull is about 6 feet (2 meters) long. The crocodile's skull is about 20 inches (51 centimeters) long.

# How Do Today's Crocodiles Measure Up?

Today: Australian freshwater crocodile

0 1 2 3 4 5 6 7 8 9 10 feet

Today: American crocodile

0 1 2 3 4 5 6 7 8 9 10 11 12 13 14 15 16 17 18 19 20 f

110 million years ago: SuperCroc

0 1 2 3 4 5 6 7 8 9 10 11 12 13 14 15 16 17 18 19 20

Key: 1 foot= 0.31 meters

SuperCroc was one of the largest crocodile relatives ever to roam the Earth. Today, there are about 12 different species, or types, of crocodiles. One is the American crocodile living in the waters along the southeastern United States and Central and South America. Another is the Australian crocodile living in the freshwaters of northern Australia. How do these crocodiles measure up to their ancient relative, SuperCroc?

21 22 23 24 25 26 27 28 29 30 31 32 33 34 35 36 37 38 39 40 ft

The biggest crocodile today weighs about 2,200 pounds (990 kilograms). SuperCroc weighed about 18,000 pounds (8,100 kilograms).

# Chapter 4

# Gulp! SuperCroc's Dinner

SuperCroc had 132 sharp teeth. Its jaws were huge. Sereno and Barr imagined that SuperCroc's bite was very powerful. When SuperCroc grabbed prey with its strong jaws and sharp teeth, the animals could not escape. How could the scientists know just how strong SuperCroc was?

They used tools to measure how hard crocodiles today can bite. Some crocodiles are strong enough to capture large animals.

◀ Most crocodiles have cone-shaped teeth that they use to hold onto and tear apart their prey.

If an animal less than half the size of SuperCroc could bite so hard, then SuperCroc could bite even harder. The scientists think that a giant crocodile like SuperCroc could probably capture a big dinosaur.

So, just what did SuperCroc eat? Scientists think SuperCroc ate just about anything it wanted. It would eat fish, turtles, or dinosaurs.

SuperCroc hunted its prey by waiting quietly under the water, with just its eyes showing above the surface. When an animal came close, SuperCroc would jump out of its watery hiding place and attack it. Then SuperCroc would pull the prey into the water. The prey would soon drown. It would be SuperCroc's dinner.

Scientists measure the bite force of a crocodile with a "bite bar."

Because adult SuperCrocs were so huge and strong, scientists believe other animals left them alone. SuperCroc probably did have fights with large dinosaurs. But SuperCrocs had an armorlike covering to protect them. Huge plates of bone, each one foot (30 cm) long, covered the creature's back.

Paul Sereno speaks at the opening of the SuperCroc exhibit at the National Geographic Society in Washington, D.C.

SARCOSUCHUS IMPERATOR

# SuperCroc on Display

There are no SuperCrocs alive today. Like dinosaurs, these giant beasts died out millions of years ago. No one really knows what happened to them. But thanks to the work of scientists, we know a lot about SuperCrocs and what they might have looked like.

Like a dentist, a student in a lab at the University of Chicago carefully drills bits of sandstone from teeth in SuperCroc's mouth.

In 2002, a model of SuperCroc was exhibited at Chicago's Museum of Science and Industry. It was displayed along with the original fossil skull Paul Sereno and his team uncovered in the African desert. Later, other museums displayed models of the giant crocodile. A traveling SuperCroc exhibit may even be coming to your town. See for yourself why this croc is so super.

A crowd gathers around a SuperCroc exhibit at the Australian Museum in Sydney.

Paul Sereno grasps the teeth from a skeletal plaster model of SuperCroc.

# How to Write an A+ Report

## 1. Choose a topic.

- Find something that interests you.

- Make sure it is not too big or too small.

## 2. Find sources.

- Ask your librarian for help.

- Use many different sources: books, magazine articles, and Web sites.

## 3. Gather information.

- Take notes. Write down the big ideas and interesting details.

- Use your own words.

## 4. Organize information.

- Sort your notes into groups that make sense.

- Make an outline. Put your groups of notes in the order you want to write your report.

## 5. Write your report.

- Write an introduction that tells what the report is about.

- Use your outline and notes as you write to make sure you say everything you want to say in the order you want to say it.

- Write an ending that tells about your report.

- Write a title.

## 6. Revise and edit your report.

- Read your report to make sure it makes sense.

- Read it again to check spelling, punctuation, and grammar.

## 7. Hand in your report!

# Glossary

| | |
|---|---|
| **ancient** | very old or describing something that lived a long time ago |
| **carnivores** | animals that eat meat |
| **desert** | a dry, sandy place that gets very little rain |
| **dig** | a search for fossil remains |
| **estimate** | to make a good guess |
| **expert** | someone who knows a lot about a subject |
| **fossil** | the hardened remains of a living thing that died millions of years ago |
| **paleontologist** | a scientist who studies fossils |
| **prey** | an animal eaten by another animal |
| **reptile** | a cold-blooded animal, such as a snake, lizard, or crocodile, with a spine and scaly skin |
| **species** | a group of animals or other living things that are alike in many ways |

# Further Reading

## • Books •

Barrett, Paul. *National Geographic Dinosaurs.* Washington, D.C.: National Geographic Society, 2001. Grades 3 & Up, 192 pages.

National Geographic. *Reptiles & Amphibians* (My First Pocket Guide). Washington, D.C.: National Geographic Society, 2001. Grades 1–5, 80 pages.

Sereno, Paul C. *SuperCroc: Paul Sereno's Dinosaur Eater* (Fossil Hunters). New York: Bearport Publishing, 2006. Grades 2–4, 32 pages.

Sloan, Christopher. *SuperCroc and the Origin of Crocodiles.* Washington, D.C.: National Geographic Society, 2002. Grades 5 & Up, 64 pages.

Walker, Sally M. *SuperCroc Found* (On My Own Science). Minneapolis: Millbrook Press, 2006. Grades 2–5, 48 pages.

## • Web Sites •

Florida Museum of Natural History
www.flmnh.ufl.edu/cnhc/

National Geographic Society
www.nationalgeographic.com/supercroc

National Geographic for Kids
http://magma.nationalgeographic.com/ngexplorer/0203/articles/mainarticle.html

Project Exploration
www.supercroc.org/

# Index

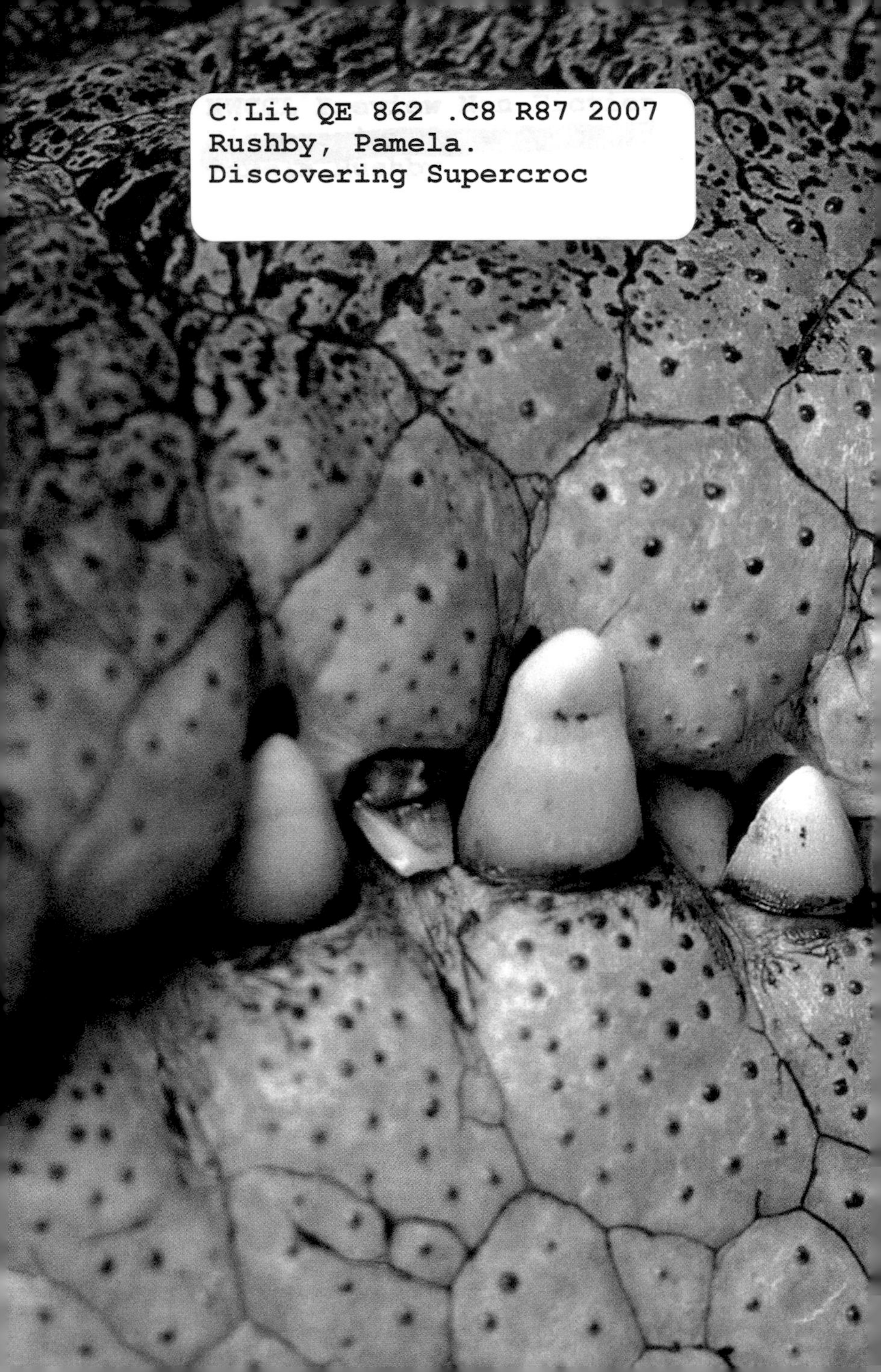